Made in the USA
Monee, IL
07 October 2021

79549424R00070